REFINED

TURNING PAIN INTO PURPOSE

TODD STOCKER
(Discussion Guide Included)
copyright <u>ToddStocker.com</u> -- all rights reserved.
Duplication of this ebook in any form is prohibited without the expressed consent of the author.

© Todd Stocker. 2011 All rights reserved. No portion of this book may be reproduced, stored in a retrieval system, or transmitted in any form or by any means -- electronic, mechanical, photocopy, recording, or any other -- except for a brief quotation in printed reviews, without the prior permission of the publisher.

Published by Cannon River Press, a division of Todd Stocker.com, P.O. Box 25946, St. Paul, MN, 55125

All Scripture quotations, unless otherwise indicated, are taken from The Holy Bible, New International Version (NIV). Copyright © 1973, 1978, 1984, International Bible Society. Used by permission of Zondervan Bible Publishers. Other Scripture references are from the following sources: The King James Version of the Bible (KJV). The Message (MSG), copyright © 1993. Used by permission of NavPress Publishing Group. The Holy Bible, New Living Translation (NLT), copyright © 1996. Used by permission of Tyndale House Publishers, Inc., Wheaton, Illinois 60189. All rights reserved.

ISBN-13: 978-1456590529
ISBN-10: 1456590529

Malachi 3

"See, I will send my messenger, who will prepare the way before me. Then suddenly the Lord you are seeking will come to his temple; the messenger of the covenant, whom you desire, will come," says the LORD Almighty.

But who can endure the day of his coming? Who can stand when he appears? For he will be like a refiner's fire or a launderer's soap. He will sit as a refiner and purifier of silver; he will purify the Levites and refine them like gold and silver. Then the LORD will have men who will bring offerings in righteousness, and the offerings of Judah and Jerusalem will be acceptable to the LORD, as in days gone by, as in former years.

"So I will come near to you for judgment. I will be quick to testify against sorcerers, adulterers and perjurers, against those who defraud laborers of their wages, who oppress the widows and the fatherless, and deprive aliens of justice, but do not fear me," says the LORD Almighty."

- Malachi 3:1-5

For My Family

and all that have been or will be Refined by God through the fires of loss

Contents

ACKNOWLEDGEMENTS

1. OUR STORY (1)
    Is This Really Happening
2. ILLUMINATION (9)
    Change Your Attitude
3. HEATING (23)
    Prepare For the Journey
4. PROTECTION (35)
    Trust in His Strength
5. DEFIANCE (45)
    Surrender to the Refiner
6. LONELINESS (57)
    Look for Signs of God's Presence
7. REFLECTION (71)
    Choose to be Radiant
8. TIMING (85)
    Wait for His Unfolding Purpose
9. AND NOW... (99)
    A Word of Encouragement

DISCUSSION GUIDE (105)

OTHER BOOKS BY THE AUTHOR (119)

NOTES (121)

ACKNOWLEDGEMENTS

A HUGE AND HEFTY THANKS GOES OUT TO

The Stebbing brothers and their families -- for creating a company that honors God and that God has used to change the lives of thousands!

All of the contributors to this book -- for your stories that I've included and the ones that I haven't. Both proved valuable to this project.

The Baltes and Stebbing families for sheltering us physically and emotionally as we transitioned into our new normal.

1

OUR STORY

OUR STORY

Is This Really Happening?

On any given day in any given city, there are people who experience struggle. The homeless person who wonders if he'll survive another frozen night on the streets of Minneapolis. The financially secure woman who is tired of pretending that her marriage is healthy. The college student who fights back the urge to give in. The man who debates leaving his long-time marriage in search of his lost youth.

Struggles. Challenges. Hardships. The Bible calls them "Trials." Whatever moniker with which we're familiar, they all say the same thing. This imperfect life is filled with joys and sorrows, fulfillment and loss. We do not expect it to be this way at the start. For example, think back to when you were young (or younger). Think about the time when you saw that girl or that guy and the pilot light of love flamed up. Back then, life seemed pure, simple and exciting. Then, as that relationship began to take root, bud and grow, what was simple became complex. The more you revealed of yourself, the more vulnerable you became. The other person also took risks and life started to feel heavy. Dating. Marriage. Children. Each adding to the woven pattern of your life.

After reaching a certain point on life's timeline, everything seems to move along fine, at least for the most part. We have relationships. We have families. We have careers and activities, all part of this thing called life.

For me, this was my experience. Falling in love. Beginning a family and career and enjoying watching my kids grow and achieve. Within the past few years, I saw my youngest daughter, Maddie, develop an incredible singing voice, love for volleyball, and a giddy joy that comes with the middle-school ages. I watched my son, Nathan, fly past my music abilities as he took up and mastered the guitar, drums, and piano. I spent hours mesmerized by my oldest daughter, Makenzie, as she danced professionally at the Bay Area Houston Ballet and Theatre Company.

The gentle waves of relationships and career rolled in and out of the shoreline of my life.

Until...

In June a few years back, my 18-year-old daughter, Makenzie, and some friends from her ballet company decided to take some photos by the water for fun. She donned her leotard, secured her long, false eyelashes and headed out the door to my parent's home on Taylor Lake in Seabrook, TX -- the perfect setting to capture her graceful form. Everything went as planned.

Poised on the dock, Makenzie and her dance partner jumped and leapt and "pirouetted" (whatever that is) as the camera froze them on film against the shimmering water and wispy pink sunset. Stunning.

At the end of the evening, they headed home. As was her habit, she called me to let me know she was on her way. It was around 8:00 p.m.

"Hi Dad," she said. "I had so much fun! I love you. I'm on my way home ..."

"I love you too. See you soon," I said.

An hour passed before I noticed that I hadn't yet heard the back door slam and her announcement, "I'M HOME!" I thought, *maybe they had stopped to talk with my parents. Maybe they went out for a Jamba Juice (her favorite). Maybe she did come home after all and I didn't hear her glide upstairs to take a shower.* So, I started texting her.

"I thought you were on your way home." No response. So I tried a few minutes later.

"You know you have to work tomorrow." Again, my cell phone was silent. Odd but not completely unusual. Finally, I shot a last text to her:

"You better have a good reason for being late!"

She did.

At 8:05 that evening, only minutes after our last conversation, Makenzie and her two friends jumped into the car and headed home. Makenzie's photo partner, Aaron was driving, Makenzie sat in the passenger seat and the photographer, a friend and fellow dancer Caitlin, was in the back seat snapping pictures of the bright pink and orange sunset.

At 8:08, they stop at a red-lighted intersection on a somewhat remote roadway. Caitlin snapped another photo of a set of clouds that looked like an open doorway into heaven and a hand, palm up, as if to say, "Welcome."[i] If you see it, this picture is beautifully comforting.

Three seconds after the last picture, they turned into the intersection and were broadsided by a Ford F250 traveling at 63 miles per hour. The impact spun the car around 360 degrees across 4 lanes of traffic and sandwiched it up against another truck in the far lane heading the other way. Aaron walked away with a broken hand. Caitlin endured severe head injuries. My Makenzie, who was so full of life, who was so joyful, who was goofy and beautiful, was killed instantly.

INSTANTLY.

What do you do when your life changes so drastically and without warning? How do you deal with a God who says over and over that He is love, that His plans are good and that part of the plan is "not to harm you but give you hope and a future"?[ii]

Sparing the details, we ended up doing what all the "experts" told us *not* to do. We pulled up stakes and moved to Minnesota, a place that had always been a refuge for our family. I took a leave of absence from being a pastor and worked for a friend of mine who owns a precious metals refining company. With the upsurge in the price of precious metals, they needed another hand preparing, melting and processing the old jewelry and silverware that came through their line. My job duties were task-oriented and people-light which allowed me to think about life and cry on the spot without embarrassment.

During the times when sorrow washed over me, Bible verses would pop into my head, ones that I hadn't thought of in years.

> *"I have refined you, but not as silver is refined. Rather, I have refined you in the furnace of suffering."*

Our Story

- Isaiah 48:10 (NLT)

"But who can endure the day of his (God's) coming? Who can stand when He appears? For he will be like a refiner's fire."

- Malachi 3:2

I realized that I was experiencing in real time what biblical refining was all about! Then one day, as I was watching old silver forks succumb to the heat in the crucible, it occurred to me that what had happened to our family over the horrific past months mimicked the process of turning old metals back into beautiful jewelry. While not a perfect match, there are points along the metal-melting process that are similar to what a person experiences in loss and grief. In that crucible experience, we encounter **Illumination, Heating, Protection, Defiance, Loneliness, Reflection** and **Timing**. All of these are important and contribute to turning pain into purpose.

This book is not written by a trained psychologist or an "in the trenches" counselor. I'm just a dad whom God saw fit to write about the painful loss of his beautiful little girl.

2

ILLUMINATION

Change Your Attitude

"Consider it pure joy, my brothers, whenever you face trials of many kinds, because you know that the testing of your faith develops perseverance. Perseverance must finish its work so that you may be mature and complete, not lacking anything."
-- James 1:2-4

"There are no hopeless situations; there are only people who have grown hopeless about them."
- Clare Boothe Luce

We know the word "crucible" by two common expressions. First, the Crucible is the container in which metals or other materials are melted. Second, the Crucible is a metaphor we use for hard experiences, trials, and difficulties. But there is a third: a little-known definition that illuminates an unexpected purpose of the Crucible. The word itself, "Crucible," originally meant "night-light." Yup. Night-light. If you have youngins, the shining from their night-light is muted by Sponge-Bob, Hello Kitty or some other personification of a "non-threatening-politically-correct-run-on-biofuel" object. If you harbor a decades-long nyctophobia (fear of darkness), your night-light simply glows green from a flat panel plugin. Whatever the holding, the night-light's purpose is to pull back the dark and reveal that which couldn't be seen otherwise. The night-light's goal is to show you a lighted path in the deep of the dark so that you can find your way to where you need to go.

However, in the midst of pain and loss, it is difficult to see how it all can work out for good. When you feel robbed of joy and happiness, it doesn't feel like things could get better and we think that there's nothing we can do to relieve the pain. Someone once said, "Grief is the darkness in which we stumble around looking for light."

In 2008, Hurricane Ike ravaged the Texas coastline. Susan Wilson wrote about her experience during that devastating time:

"Within a 3 month period, I lost my job of 9 years and my home, thanks to Hurricane Ike. I shed many tears of the loss of both. More so for specific items, I lost in my home. I think the worst loss came from finding my daughter's birth to 5-year old scrapbook. I had quickly grabbed the important items but left the scrapbook when we evacuated. It was on the bottom shelf in the lowest room in my home.

ILLUMINATION

When I returned to the house, I opened the cabinet where the book was and water came out. There was the scrapbook, destroyed. Most of the items left in our house were that way. All of this brought many tears on many nights. I had people tell me they were glad it was me not them, as they were not sure they could have handled it all. I admit at times I was not sure I could handle it either. Everything was sad -- even cartoons. I cried watching Cartoons for goodness sakes!

Then I looked around me and made a choice. I chose to trust God. I knew God had a plan, and while I certainly was not sure what his plan was, I knew that he does not give you more than he knows you can handle. So, I knew I could handle it. I also knew that everything I lost was just things -- I had my family. There was nothing I lost that I could not replace. Okay, maybe I could not replace the scrapbook, but I still had the memory of making it and the memories of every day in my daughters first 5 years. I did not need a scrapbook to remind me of those awesome years. What was more important was that I had her."

Like Susan, you have a choice regarding tough life events. Either you choose to see your situation as incurable or you choose to see your situation as temporary. You can choose to stay in the Mopey Boat (as my wife calls it) or you can put your paddle in the water of pain and begin to row.

One move will lead to another and then another and eventually, you'll find yourself living *with* the consequences of the pain instead of living *in* them.

There are thousands of stories about people who entered the heat of the furnace of life, made a choice and ended up thriving instead of just surviving.

Bethany Hamilton. Bethany was a teenaged surfer who grew up loving three things: God, family, and surfing. On any given day, she would be on her board riding the swells that crashed onto the Kauai, Hawaii beaches. However, she was about to enter the crucible.

On October 31, 2003, Bethany and friends paddled out for another enjoyable day on the water. Gliding just below the waves, a 14-foot tiger shark watched Bethany position herself for the next big wave, waited for its opportunity and then it attacked. The shark clamped onto and severed Bethany's left arm, leaving her helpless in the water. After being pulled to shore, her friends quickly secured the wound and transported her to the local doctors. During the trauma, Bethany lost over 60% of her blood and faced multiple surgeries. But for her, the real potential loss was never to surf again. She was being tested, she believed and faced a choice that all of us have when we hit the walls of life. Bethany could either succumb to bitterness and depression she could choose to be positive and see that even in the midst of pain, hope can pull you through.

Bethany went on to place 5th in the Open Women's Surf competition and just over a year after the attack she took

1st place in the Explorer Women's division of the 2005 NSSA National Championships – winning her first National Title.

Chris Gardner. Being raised in a rough neighborhood of Milwaukee, Chris's early life was fraught with struggle. At age 8, his mother was convicted of trying to murder his stepfather. One day, she was there, the next she was in prison and her sudden disappearance wasn't explained to Chris or his siblings.

Throughout Chris' young life, he bounced around from foster homes to relative's houses. At the age of 18, he graduated from high school and went into the Navy. After his stint, he returned to a wife, a baby son and a job as a medical supply salesmen. For Chris, he thought his life was finally on track. Unfortunately, he lost his job and his wife walked out on him and his son leaving Chris to be a single parent. Homeless and sleeping in subway restrooms, Chris could have given up. He could have ended it all out of frustration and hopelessness. Instead, Chris knew that the hardships that he was experiencing had a purpose. He didn't know what that purpose was but he knew that the "night-light" of struggles would light the way to where he was to be.

Eventually, Chris would land a job as a stockbroker and then go on to form his own financial investment firm, Gardner Rich & Co. Today, Chris is an author, speaker, and financial giant but he recognizes that if it weren't for the crucible of struggle, he wouldn't be the success story he is today.[iii]

Donna Whitson. On January 13, 1996, Donna was going about her day when her son ran to her and told her a neighbor had just seen Donna's 9-year-old daughter, Amber, being forced into a car. A parent's worst nightmare.

Frantically, Donna called the news media and alerted the FBI. A massive searched was launched but to no avail. Four days later, Donna's precious daughter was found murdered in a storm drainage ditch. Her killer was never found.

Donna and her family were in the crucible. How could anything good come out of something so evil? Amber's family soon established People Against Sex Offenders. They collected signatures hoping to force the Texas Legislature into passing more stringent laws to protect children. That same year, the *Amber Hagerman Child Protection Act* was signed into law by President Bill Clinton.

Today, we recognize the great contribution that the AMBER Alert system has made in saving hundreds of children's lives nationally and internationally. For Donna and her family, the crucible of death showed the way to give others life.[iv]

There are countless stories like these; people who have had every reason to give up because of loss, struggle, and grief. However, they took each obstacle and dealt with it as is.

I'll bet that all of these examples cause you to ask, "How do I deal with the struggles, pain and trials that come into my life?"

Sometimes, we, in our lives, experience major potholes in the road. Death. Disease. Brokenness. Other times we deal with simple little bumps, small unexpected changes or delays. So again, "How do I deal with the struggles, pain, and trials that come into my life?" Maybe the better question is,

"How does GOD want me to deal with them?" I think there are some simple answers on our journey in turning pain into purpose.

1. Change your attitude about trials.

Generally, men react to stress with anger and women react to stress with sadness. Men take out the lawn mower and try to fire it up after a long winter in the garage. After several hard pulls, it sputters momentarily and goes back into hibernation mode. In frustration and anger, we kick the thing and go inside! Women juggle family, home and often a career. But if something goes wrong in the schedule, the bottom lip starts to quiver and tears flow. Generally, that's how we are wired.

We can change our attitude about trials. How? One word – Choose. Choose to react positively and not negatively to every situation. Choose to rearrange your perspective to see struggles as formative and not destructive. Choose to anticipate the opportunity inherent in every frustration. Even though you may not feel like it, choosing is an act of the mind. The New Living Translation of James 1:2 says,

*"Dear brothers and sisters, whenever trouble comes your way, let it be an **opportunity** for joy!"*
- James 1:2 (NLT)

Have you ever thought of difficult times as an opportunity? Some of us naturally react to trials positively, seeing them as grand opportunities for growth. Most of us, however, react negatively. We impatiently see hardships and frustrations as undeserved and unfair. Even thinking, "If God loved me, He wouldn't have allowed this to happen!" Maybe we should say, "*Because* God loves me, He allowed this to happen!" It's not easy to do and, as they say, attitude is everything! If you react negatively to trials, dust yourself off and try again.

2. **Turn your focus on the One who is in charge of your hard times.**

No, that's not a typo. God is the one who gives or allows the trials and the stresses in your life. The Bible says that all things are subject to God's power. It also says that everything that exists is under the watchful eye of the Creator. If you believe that God is in complete control, then you have to believe that whatever we experience in this life is first filtered through the fingers of God.

There are several venues through which God gives or allows difficulties in our lives.

Trials come by means of consequences. When you don't eat right or exercise, eventually, the consequence is poor health. If you don't prepare for a presentation at work or a test at school, the consequence is a bad review. God has built in consequences for poor behavior.

Trials come as a result of a sinful world. The world is broken. It is not running at top capacity. Because we live day to day in a tainted world, eventually we are faced with hardships that we can't control.

Trials come as a result of Satan and his spiritual forces. Satan will do anything he can to break your desire for God.

When we get flooded with the enemy's assault, that's called 'temptation' and it comes from Satan but is allowed by God.

Trials come directly from God. Mostly, the trials that God gives are designed to bring someone into a deeper relationship with Him. He is not content to let His children wander away. He will pursue you if you choose to sin and He will use trials to bring you back. This is usually called "Hitting Rock Bottom."

A friend of mine's daughter chose to turn from her upbringing and run with a difficult crowd. After months and months of trying to help her see the wrong she was doing, my friend's prayer changed from "God, please help her" to "God, please make her situation and consequences worse." Amazing! God answered that prayer by giving his daughter horrible experiences as she lived on the street. Eventually, she did "hit rock bottom" and is on her way to living a fulfilling life -- closer to God and closer to her family.

God uses these sources as part of His plan for us. He is the one who is in control of our suffering. Do we know why? No. Do we know how it's going to turn out? No. Is there a purpose in the trials that we go through? Yes. Do we know what that purpose is? Yes!

Remember James 1:2? It says that when troubles come, it is an opportunity for joy! It is an opportunity to be taught. It is an opportunity for us to be strengthened in all aspects of our lives. It is an opportunity for us to point to the LORD and say, "He is the one who has allowed this difficult time to come upon me and He is the One in whom I put my trust!"

When faced with a mountain in our path, many of us focus first on how to move it! We analyze what happened, what went wrong, how are we going to get out of this mess, how are we going to make it through. That thought process is helpful but too many times we jump right into decision making rather than focusing on the Creator of that 'mountain' in the first place! He will first give you comfort in the struggle; second, give you insight on how to solve problems or endure pain; and third, create hope that it will all work out.

Hope is life-giving. Hope is freeing. Hope is motivating because it tells you that everything is going to be okay. It picks you up after a hard fall. It gives you energy when you feel exhausted. Hope drives the confidence you need in the Crucibles of life. The Bible says,

> *"We know how troubles can develop passionate patience in us, and how that patience, in turn, forges the tempered steel of virtue, keeping us alert for whatever God will do next. In alert expectancy such as this, we're never left feeling shortchanged."[v]*
>
> *- Romans 5:3-4 (MSG)*

In short, God's Spirit gives us a hope-filled perspective in the times of pain and loss.

That is the perspective that God Himself has when he allows pain in our lives. He sees the finish line of our grief. He knows that struggle is necessary to form us into the people He wants us to be, even though we want it to go away. During the process of refining, He never leaves us to the whims of the flames of tragedy.

We want to be comfortable, God wants purpose. We want the easy life, God desires meaning. It's ironic that the violent Crucible is also the guiding night-light through our pain. The loss of your job should cause you to tailspin (darkness), but God uses it to show you that He will provide all your needs (light: see Matthew 6:25-27). The crumbling of a relational bond should force the grip of depression to squeeze the life out of you (darkness), but God uses it to reassure you that He will never leave (light: see Joshua 1:5). The unexpected death of your daughter causes you to freeze up with despair, sadness, and pain (darkness), but God uses it to show you that even in the Crucible, He is still in control (light: see Romans 8:28).

The Crucible. The night-light for your purpose. The night-light for His Love. That harsh tool in the hands of a gentle Refiner gives you the hope that it's going to be okay.

3

HEATING

HEATING

Prepare for the Journey

"I have told you these things, so that in me you may have peace. In this world you will have trouble. But take heart! I have overcome the world." -- John 16:33

"When you're in the midst of tragedy, it's too late to prepare for it. God prepares us now for what is to come."
- Pastor Steve Riggle, Grace Church, Houston TX

The Lord uses every experience in our lives to reveal something about ourselves. For His purpose, He uses difficulties to shape and form us into the people He wants us to be. Someone stated, *"Character is formed in the crucible of adversity."* Great line. Wish I'd penned it, especially since it is the crucible with which we deal every day.

When I was a refiner, one of the most important lessons I learned was that of the Heat. At the beginning of my day, I'd have to fire up the furnaces to make sure that they are hot enough to handle the work of melting. Gold melts at around 1950 degrees F so it took around half an hour just to get the furnaces up to that temperature. If the heat of the furnace is less, the metal would only be ruined for future use or, at the least, have to go through the violent process of remelting. Preparing the Heat is an important step in God's refining process.

A few weeks before the accident that claimed our daughter's life, our family attended a worship service at a church whose pastor and wife were kidnapped in the Philippines while doing mission work. The powerful series was called "Caught in the Crossfire."[vi] The message that morning dealt with being ready for what life may bring. He spoke about the suffering servant, Job, who had his life all set up for retirement; cash, kids, real estate, property, good relationships and a strong love for God. Even with all the blessings, the Lord allowed Satan to storm into Job's life and take everything he had. Without any notice, Job lost his animals, property, children and even his health. The pastor made the point that Job had no idea this was coming. After all, Job was a man who loved God even more than anything, even his 'stuff.' The pastor then made a point that opened my eyes to what God had been doing in me. He said that when you are in the midst of a tragedy, it's too late to prepare for it.

Isn't that true? Even in everyday life, there are examples of that truth. You're driving to work and you get a flat tire. If you don't have a spare or even a tire wrench, you're going nowhere. You're out on a run and even though there was forecast for rain, you decide to chance it. Soon, you find yourself sloshing through a downpour and you're still a few miles from home without the proper gear.

Heating

When you look around and find that you're in the furnace of frustration and pain, you can't hit the pause button and get what you need to survive it.

Colleen, one of the bloggers in my community, commented on the suddenness of tragedy.

"Over my lifetime, I really didn't experience intense heat and I guess I just bubbled along feeling relatively secure in my walk with God. As a lifelong Christian -- attending parochial school, weekly church, Sunday School, fairly regular prayer life, confirmed, married in the church, all my children baptized -- I guess I never felt the need for too much change. Then boom! Out of nowhere, our world was rocked by tragedy. No more Pollyanna worldview. Bad things DO happen. It was a very intense and life-changing time. To be honest, not all in a good way -- at least not from what I see right now." Colleen Hicks

There are different levels of intensity when it comes to life's difficulties. Some are inconveniences. Some are frustrations. Some are obstacles and some are real trials. Some of the pain that we experience in life is completely out of our control and some of it is self-inflicted.

I remember as a kid, learning a new word from one of my seedier friends at school. This word is on the 'naughty list' but it fits well with the classic song, "Chitty, Chitty, Bang, Bang!" And yes, that is the song that I sang -- bad word inserted -- all the way home from school that day. As I rounded the corner into our cul-de-sac, one of our neighbors happened to be out front gardening. Immediately she called my mom and informed her of my interesting song lyric. In turn, my mother met me out front and said, "Todd. Do you know that *that* word is one we don't say. It is a very naughty word and you need to stop using it or else there will be consequences."

She was lovingly firm and the message came across loud and clear. However, I liked how *that word* sounded and how it fit well with the sing-song that was hopping around in my head. So, instead of obeying my mom, who had disappeared back inside the house, I chose to launch into another and even louder chorus.

Dogs started barking. Neighbors came out with pitchforks and shovels. Bats flapped violently from leafless trees. OK, I'm exaggerating but it was a dark point when my mom stormed out of the front door, grabbed me by the back collar and dragged me directly to THE ROOM. Yes. You know which about which room I'm talking. The Bathroom.

I took my position with my head bent over the sink as my mom grabbed the bar of soap. Holding it up, she said what every parent says before they discipline their child, "This is going to hurt me more than it hurts you!"

As I saw the look of determination on her face and her white knuckles clenching the Dove, a demonic voice crackled from my lips and I muttered, "You're a LIAR!" Not one of my banner days of communication.

God allowed that pain in my life for a reason, for a purpose. That purpose on that day was for me to learn first, not to disobey my mom and second, not ever to buy bars of Dove soap!

In preparation for the Heat of pain, each one of us has to settle this question in our minds, "Is God for me or against me." If He is against me, I don't have to look far to prove it. Loss, struggle, pain, disappointment, it's all there. But if He's for me, then everything that I experience in life, the good, the bad and the ugly, is for an ultimate reason or purpose. My Bible says God *is* on my side, that He *is* working behind the scenes of the tragic losses of my life, that He *is* taking the broken pieces of my life and creating an incredible work of art. The Bible says,

> *"And we know that in **all things** God works **for the good** of those who love him, who have been called according to his purpose."*
>
> *- Romans 8:28*

We don't know what tomorrow holds but there are simple ways to prepare for life's journey in the wilderness. Using a hiking metaphor, here are 5 practices to help you be prepared.

1. Get to know the tour guide.

There were so many lessons our family learned when we went white-water rafting in Colorado several years ago. We'd never done it before so we had no idea what we were in for. During our training, the three most important rules were: 1) Listen to the guide. 2) Listen to the guide. 3) Yup, you guessed it, listen to the guide. Paddles could break, the raft could sink but if we kept listening to Steve (our guide on that trip), we'd be ok.

As you journey in life, the most important practice is to listen to and get to know the Lord. He is not just a guide, but He is your Creator. He knows how much you can handle and how much you can't. He knows how you react to situations and already has a plan to strengthen you in the weakness of your life. As the Bible says, He is your loving Father and what loving father would allow pain in a child's life unless it was for a better and greater purpose?

How do you get to know your Guide? Keep reading.

2. Study the map. Study it again -- and again -- and again.

It was early Saturday morning when a group of fathers and sons gathered for a hike through the White Tank Mountains in Arizona where I pastored. As the organizer, I figured we'd take the short two-mile hike with the kiddos and then stop for breakfast on the way back. Simple.

However, I assumed that the trail would be easily marked out and that it would be flat and straight. Wrong. We began our hike without any map and only a vague idea of the movings of the route. What was intended to be a 45-minute jaunt turned out to be a 5-hour journey. I took a left when I should have taken a right. I didn't study a map.

The Word of God is our map. It gives us direction on who we are, what to do, where to go and how to respond. It tells us about our Guide who counted His Son lost so that we could be found. It shapes our thinking and perspective so that when we encounter the wilderness, we can remain calm and not be overwhelmed. Study the map.

3. Make a plan.

A healthy organization always has a plan. Mission and vision statements guide it. Core values and goals inform it. They know how to navigate ups and downs in the market because they have a plan -- or at least they have a general idea of how they'll handle 'tough times.'

Do you have a plan for your life or are you simply going day to day wondering what's coming next. If God were to suddenly call home someone whom you love, would you know when and how to grieve? Would you know how to recognize the signs of depression? Having a plan simply says, "When trials come my way, I will choose to (*fill in the blank*)."

It may be "… I will choose to find the lesson in it." "I will choose to allow myself to cry in public." "I will choose to spend quiet time with God or with others." Make a plan because, as Pastor Steve Riggle says, *"When you're in the midst of tragedy, it's too late to prepare for it."*

4. Gather supplies.

During a dry spell in my ministry, a friend of mine suggested that I start an 'encouragement file'. It is a simple folder in my desk drawer that has encouraging scripture, emails, notes, and quotes that shine light and perspective when I can't see daily joy. In it, I have a letter from a family who I helped when they lost a child. I have quotes from authors like Francis Chan and Max Lucado. The most precious item is a little paper bible that my daughter made me when I was thinking of quitting the church I was serving. She gave it to me and said, "This is so you'll like being a pastor again."

Precious.

These are supplies for my journey. I have many others and they keep me grounded when I feel like my life is floating away. They make my heart sing instead of cuss. They help me find focus when I can't see. For me, this supply pack has helped me on the journey from pain to purpose.

Some people don't use an encouragement file but instead, they pack a journal. Filled with their thoughts, memories, and ideas, their journal is a story of strength, wandering and victory through which they find encouragement. Whether it's an encouragement file or a journal, find "supplies" that will help you when you run into a dead end.

5. Hike together.

Never go it alone. No matter what hiking program you're on, this is the mantra that is drilled into you. Never go it alone.

It reminds me of when I joined our church's men's group on a hike through the Boundary Waters in Northern Minnesota. Rugged and remote, navigating the terrain can be tough especially if you're portaging from one lake to another with a 125-pound canoe balancing on your shoulders. But because I was one of the youngest in the group, I thought that I didn't need to wait for the "old men" of the group and I forged on. After 15 minutes, I was well ahead of the group and puffed up with pride. Just as I was thinking how great I was, my foot slipped and I fell to my knees. The heavy canoe that was balancing on my shoulders lunged forward and its pointed nose lodged in the thick mud just ahead of me. I was stuck. I couldn't move and I was all alone.

Several minutes later, the rest of the group caught up with me. One of the elders commented that I look like a pathetic Atlas carrying the world on my shoulders. I felt like a goof. To drive home the point of never go it alone, they walked right by me, leaving me to suffer a few moments more and then came back to relieve my pain and my pride.

With whom do you hike? Do you have people who are walking with you on the journey of life or are you stubbornly thinking you can go it alone? When struggles and trials threaten to get you stuck, who do you call to help you get perspective and share the burden?[vii]

I suggest that if you're not plugged into a faith community, that you make that a priority. At a minimum, find people who know you or you'd like to get to know and develop deeper relationships. When you do, not only are you more equipped to handle life, but you can be a blessing to them in return.

Being prepared makes the difference between surviving and thriving during times of difficulty. The beauty is that God leads us in that process. For years, unknown to us, God had been preparing us for the tragic loss of our daughter. He knew when she was born and when she was to die. So a long time ago, God moved Kellie and me to begin our days reading about this God who says He loves us. We learned about this "Divine Mentor" who opened our eyes to His power and grace. We comprehended the fact that God is on our side. We understood that God had defeated death through the sacrifice of His Son. Our daughter, Makenzie knew it as well.

At the time of our tragedy, we knew Who was in charge and to Whom we needed to turn. We knew God's character, His ability, and His heart. We had friends who surrounded us and kept reminding us that Makenzie was alive in heaven because Jesus had changed her heart. We knew she believed in Him as her Savior. We also knew that God is a god who wastes nothing, that this seemingly random accident has a purpose that is unfolding in the lives of all who knew Makenzie.

In all of it, the words from Job 1:21 rang through,

"The LORD gave and the LORD has taken away; may the name of the LORD be praised."
- *Job 1:21*

We don't need to ask the "why" questions because God told us that His grace is enough. We don't need to spiral down into the cold darkness of depression because God showed us the warm light of His love. Our strength, in the middle of our loss, had been realized *before* Makenzie's death on June 3rd and He carries and guides us day by day, moment by moment.

4

PROTECTION

Trust in His Strength

"Now the Lord had arranged for a great fish to swallow Jonah. And Jonah was inside the fish for three days and three nights." -- Jonah 1:7 (NLT)

"Develop an attitude of gratitude, and give thanks for everything that happens to you, knowing that every step forward is a step toward achieving something bigger and better than your current situation." -- Brian Tracy

The furnace sounds like a jet engine. It roars. It hisses, waiting to be fed, eager to consume anything that it is given. And it will. Linger too long in the furnace and even the Crucible meets a cruel end which enlightens an ironic purpose of the Crucible.

Protection.

Without the Crucible, the metal is doomed. Left to fight the furnace on its own, the silver and gold would be liquefied into a useless pile of slag. But within the Crucible, the Refiner can control the amount and intensity of the heat that the metal experiences. Albeit a cruel and violent tool, the

Crucible protects the metal from certain uselessness if not obliteration.

Reminds me of Jonah. You know the story. God asked Jonah to deliver a message to the evil people of Nineveh -- a message revealing their sin and calling them to repentance. Jonah gave in to his fear, hoped on a ship and sailed in the opposite direction of that wretched city. God sent a storm to rock the boat and, fearing for their lives, the others threw Jonah into the waters, thinking it was his fault. The bible then says that the Lord provided a great fish or a whale to swallow Jonah (Jonah 1:7). Did you catch that? God *provided* a whale. When I provide someone with something it is to help them out in someway. God provided this whale to help Jonah and not to harm him.

Without the whale, Jonah would have certainly drowned. The storm waves would have kept him under and the currents would have brought Jonah to his doom. But God's plans rule. There is nothing we can do to stop them. So God used a creature of nature to swallow Jonah to protect him from certain death. I don't think Jonah saw it that way but nevertheless, the truth that is revealed is this; that which was intended for harm ultimately was provided for good.

As difficult as it may seem right now, the pain you're experiencing might be keeping you from a worse disaster down the road. God might be setting up a roadblock in your life because the path you want to go down leads to a cliff.

It reminds me of when my son's frisbee went out into the street. He immediately ran after it, not thinking, not looking and not seeing the car that was motoring his way. I happened to be standing by the street and as he ran by, I abruptly

PROTECTION

grabbed his little arm, stopping him mid-stride. When it was all said and done, he walked away with a bruised arm from my grip but he still walked away. My firm but hurtful grasp protected him from meeting face-to-grill with a 4,000-pound car.

The concept of God hurting us to protect us is a difficult one to grasp. In fact, this is a common objection to faith for people I speak with. Usually, the objection begins, "If God were so good and loving how could He let (fill-in the blank) happen!" Sometimes I have an answer, especially if it is a few months down the road from the incident. Many times, I'm left to say "I don't know, but let me tell you what I do know." Then I speak about a God who is always in control and has a good purpose in mind even though we might not know what it is right now. And that is where trust comes in.

Robin's young daughter, Haley, was to undergo intensive brain surgery to remove a cancerous tumor. The doctors told her that the chances of survival were small and that she'd better be prepared for the possibility of Haley not surviving the surgery. Immediately, Robin called on people to pray for her little girl.

A few days before the surgery, Robin sent out this prayer email:

"I put two tired little girls to bed last night at 7:45. I had 'let' my boy go and play with his friends at the auto show. So I found myself alone in a quiet house. As I often feel like doing after the girls are sound asleep and -- if I'm not also wiped out next to one or both of them -- I felt like getting comfortable and

39

sharing some time with a friend. I wasn't sure which I felt like doing but a few things came to mind. I could read a chapter in a book I have, entitled "Why bad things happen to good people," I could open up the Bible to any page and see what was in store for me that evening, or I could work on a study I'd been involved with before Haley's diagnoses but which I have since been neglecting. I felt pulled toward the study guide.

So I got snuggled into bed, set my Bible beside me, and opened the workbook on my lap. I started reading. The words jumped off the page because it seemed to apply to our family's current situation. Then I got to a page with a bold title. It read 'Carrie's Cancer'. Could I really go on? Did I want to continue? I have a tendency to run from difficult situations. The urge was strong. But I took a deep breath and kept going. The author's daughter had an experience with cancer when she was young. He mentioned a passage in scripture that had spoken to their family. It was John 11:4 when Jesus said, 'This sickness will not end in death. No, it is for God's glory so that God's Son may be glorified through it.'

I felt a mixture of hope and despair because in a flash, I saw that this could mean two things. Either God is telling me that Haley will not die and that

Protection

God's using this trial in her life to renew His presence in your lives; or that even though she dies here on earth, she'll live on eternally in Heaven, safe and sound and incredibly loved by the Father. Either way, they both bring me comfort. I selfishly don't want to lose her, but I think God wants us all to know that she's guarded and will be ok. He has her. Whether He lets her live here with us or takes her with Him, He has her. Who better to take care of that baby?!

After reading John 11:4, another verse popped into my head, Joshua 1:9 '...be strong and courageous. Do not be terrified; do not be discouraged, for the Lord your God will be with you wherever you go.' And then I flipped back a page and read Joshua 1:5 '...I will be with you; I will never leave you nor forsake you.' I didn't read each word to find these passages. They leapt out at me.

Because of what it says in John 11:4, '...so that God's Son may be glorified through it,' I am sharing this experience with you. I'm hoping it will be of some encouragement to all of you who love Haley and have been praying for her. She's going to be ok. No matter what.

There are so many tragic things happening every second of every day all around this world. There are troops suffering and dying in the cold mountains away from their homes, there are people diagnosed and dying of terminal illnesses, there are unspeakable things happening in individual homes, there are lonely and desperate people crying out in despair to God. It was an overwhelming and depressing revelation. And I wonder if there were an equal number of people praising God, lifting up His name, thanking Him. I hoped so. Before you pray for our situation, please first thank God for all the wonderful things He's done. Whatever that is in your lives. Please, before you pray for Haley, please remember to give God praise.

God's at work. We're not going through this alone. And there's a reason for this. I once wrote down what I feel is my life's motto: 'Sometimes I've preferred ignorance over knowledge because I often prefer bliss over chaos.' It fits me so well. I'm neither proud nor ashamed of it. Just accepting of it.

A couple of months ago, I read in the Bible somewhere that, if we ask for wisdom, we'd better be prepared to handle it. I'd been asking for wisdom and clarity up until that point. Then I took a step back. I'm not so sure I want to or have to know what God's up to. Not right now. Maybe I'll just let Him take control. It takes an incredible weight off my shoulders."

PROTECTION

Robin's faith in the Lord strengthened her for the upcoming trial. She trusted that God would protect Haley, even if it meant bringing her to heaven. She knew that the next weeks, months and years were going to be difficult and she was surrendered.

Today, Haley is a wonderful young gal who is full of life. God had a purpose in mind and, while difficult, the trial of surgery and recovery proved to be a good thing.

Reminds me of the Biblical story of Shadrach, Meshach, and Abednego.[viii] They were three young lads, captured by the horrid King Nebuchadnezzar and forced into slavery. When the king demanded that everyone bow down and worship an image of his god, the three boys refused. They were followers of the Lord. They were devoted to the God of Abraham, Isaac, and Jacob and they were ready for any consequence that the king might impose on them for their disobedience.

Angered, the king ordered that they be thrown into a raging hot furnace. But when the king looked into the flames, Shadrach Meshach, and Abednego were walking around, unbound and unharmed. They had been protected from the blaze of the furnace. Not only that, but an angel was accompanying them. God was in control. He protected them in the fire and even the King was amazed.

There are other stories in the Bible of God's protection. Moses leading the Israelites and being guided by God's pillar of clouds by day and protected by His pillar of fire at night. (Isn't it interesting that God used FIRE to protect them). Daniel in the Lion's Den. The disciples in the fierce storm. Paul escaping from angry crowds. And all of these accounts teach the same lessons: God is in control and we can be grateful that He turns pain into purpose.

Right now, you or someone you cherish may be facing a life-threatening situation. Cancer that was diagnosed in late stages. An accident that leaves you hospitalized. A pregnancy that is deteriorating the health of both mother and child. Whatever the alarm, God know's how much heat it takes to accomplish His purpose and He knows how little strength you have left.

For some reason, the fire through which you are walking is perfectly managed by God. He knows your strength limit. Ironic, isn't it. When you feel at your weakest, that is actually a sign of God's strength. When you sense a loss of energy and deeper feelings of depression, it is then that God activates an extra amount of His Grace that is required for your survival.

No matter how difficult the Crucible of our loss has been, my Refiner is still in control. No matter how brutal, ruthless or slow, the Crucible is an agonizing gift that is melting, molding and making you into something that your Refiner can really use.

Protection

5

DEFIANCE

Protection

Surrender to the Refiner

"Going a little ahead, Jesus fell on his face, praying, 'My Father, if there is any way, get me out of this! But please, not what I want. You, what do you want?'"
- *Matthew 26:39 (MSG)*

"He who rejects change is the architect of decay. The only human institution which rejects progress is the cemetery." --
Harold Wilson

Because I'm human, I stand defiant against change. Knowing who's behind it all, I sometimes grab Him by the tie, pull Him towards me over the table, stare Him right in the eye and mumble, "Go ahead and try to change me!" He simply smiles, puts on His goggles and heat shield, and lowers me into the Crucible.

From inside, I still stand straight, like a fork; prongs pointing skyward; trying to show that I'm not going to melt. Even as my Savior Refiner is setting me gently into the roar of the blazing furnace, I stand in defiance against the heat; refusing to bend; refusing to change; refusing to give in.

I am arrogant; I am foolish.

If you were to watch me in the Crucible, you would see me start to sweat. You would see my prongs begin to curl. You would see me — still defiant — tilt to one side and then disappear beneath the rim of the Crucible.

I am melted; I am undone. And my Savior Refiner is still in control.

If the plated forks fight the melt, they are skimmed off and deemed useless but eventually, every piece of metal that enters the Crucible is subject to this process. Once useful, then useless, then defiant, then changed, then useful again. It is a good process, yet harsh. It is one that my humanness does not desire nor seek out. Yet it is the only way.

He packed his bag for another day of work. His was a calling and he was a professional -- the best in the business. He knew the stakes were high and the payoff was handsome. For many years, he had dealt with rebels and traitors to his government and he knew where they'd be hiding. He took another glance at his orders and smiled. *When I catch this cell of terrorists, I might be able to retire*, He thought.

With an extra bounce in his step, he joined his team and headed toward the small town. Nothing would deter him from completing his mission. Nothing except …

According to his calculations, the town was just over the hill a few hundred yards away. His pace quickened as his sense of determination grew. Suddenly, a bright light stopped

Saul and his posse in their tracks. Too bright to be a lantern. Too direct to be a casual fire. It was a light like none other and Saul knew that he couldn't escape for it surrounded them on all sides.

As recounted in Acts 9,

> *"He fell to the ground and heard a voice say to him, 'Saul, Saul, why do you persecute me?'*
>
> *'Who are you, Lord?' Saul asked.*
>
> *'I am Jesus, whom you are persecuting,' He replied. 'Now get up and go into the city, and you will be told what you must do.'"*
>
> *- Acts 9:4-6*

From this point on, Saul (whose name God changed to Paul) became a powerful tool in the Refiner's hand through which the message of hope in Jesus was deployed -- even reaching into our lives today some 2000 plus years later.

God leads and directs. According to His purpose and plan, events happen and don't happen. They serve as the ebb and flow to our lives. All the while, He is in control. In fact, there is nothing that we can ever encounter that doesn't filter first through the fingertips of our Almighty LORD! Every hurt and pleasure. Every pain and joy. They all are under the supervising eye of God.

If this is true (which it is), that means that no matter how hard the situation, God is still in control of it all. And if God is always in control (which He is), that means that there is a reason -- a purpose -- for that which keeps us up at night. It means that the pink-slip in the mail, the late-night call from your child, the prognosis over the phone is encompassed by the watchful gaze of the Lord.

We are fine with this truth as long as life is going fine. I'm sure that even Saul, before his conversion, believed that all was well. But when life gets hard, we push and rebel and remain defiant against our God who knows best. We are defiant because there is the hope that we can push back fear. We are defiant because there is a need for being in control. We are defiant because we are not used to and do not like the inevitable elements of change because change involves loss and we hate that. David Osborn said:

"Too often we try to use God to change our circumstances, while he is using our circumstances to change us."

This truth is so difficult for most to grasp. To think that the 'Big Guy Upstairs' could stop the tragedies in life but chooses not to is, for some, inconceivable. Even the strongest of the faithful can be shaken to their core when our good God lets evil have its way in a person's life.

At a point in my college career, I attended an ethics class at Arizona State University. It was a trying experience. Not because the coursework was exceptionally difficult or exhaustive but because the professor took every occasion to point out the seeming contradictions between the Bible and real life. Some of his rantings talked about the fallacy of religion in general but especially Christianity, calling it a belief system based on the mythology of curious minds.

After several weeks, I decided to talk with him after class -- not to confront him but to find out his story. As we talked, it because desperately clear that at one point, he was a solid, Bible-believing Christ-follower who knew scripture. I finally asked him, "What is it that offends you about God?" A stone cold and rather distant look crept over his face and without blinking an eye, he replied, "What kind of loving God would take away my 2-year-old daughter from me?"

He had had an experience of loss. The tragic murder of his daughter caused a death in him as well. He was defiant. Standing hard against the heat of loss, against the hand of the Refiner. His life changed yet he was refusing to surrender and melt into the new normal that loss and grief creates.

That was over twenty years ago and sometimes I still think about that painful conversation. And then I feel sad for him. I wonder if he had ever changed. I wonder if the Lord melted away his defiance and I wonder if his heart surrendered to the fact that God is always, always in control.

When life is good, the "God Is In Control" message is pretty simple to grasp. When life is hard and the heat of loss and change threatens to engulf you, that message is irritating. However, once the reality of God's ability to handle your situation really sinks deep into the heart of your life, everything is different. Your outlook is different. Your attitudes and stress levels change. You begin to understand and live out the fact that it's not what happened to you that matters. It is how you react to what happened to you that matters. This is an issue of perspective.

After my daughter was killed, I took time off from church-work to heal. During that time, I worked with lovely people at a refinery, processing and melting gold and silver.

(This experience served as the inspiration for this book, by the way).

There was one guy with whom I worked that stands out in memory. Mike had been in the business for many years. He knew the ins and outs of metal refining better than anyone in the state. Mike was a big husky fellow with an even bigger heart. He would move around the furnaces and crucible racks with the ease and grace of a ballerina (although I doubt I'd ever tell him that to his face).

During my early stages of learning the refining trade, I made a critical mistake. Filling an older crucible with a *brand-new-car's* worth of silver, I set it into a furnace that roared at 1600 degrees. This kind of melt takes around 25 minutes to finish -- the perfect amount of time for a quick bite to eat. So I left it there and headed for the break room. After making a sandwich and turning on ESPN, I settled in, noting the time so as to retrieve the silver melt. The minutes passed. My mind was distracted by the NFL weekend replay. Before I recognized it, 45 minutes had slipped away. Realizing the time, I bolted to the refining room, donned my protective gear and lifted the lid on the furnace. A majority of the crucible had melted away and the large volume of now liquid silver was spilled onto the floor making it mostly unusable. I couldn't believe it.

Mike had followed me in and saw the disaster. Using tongs, he quickly and quietly helped me fish out the remaining crucible parts from the heat, cleaned out the furnace and salvaged a fraction of the original silver that had poured onto the fireproof concrete floor. I was devastated. I knew he and the owners would be upset and I knew that this could cost me my job. But Mike's response changed the way I view life today. He simply said, "It's no big deal."

That was it.

Nothing deep. Nothing theological just a simple recognition that there are "bigger deals" in life and this wasn't one of them. He also knew that the owners would make sure that their customer would still get full payment for the melt even though the company would take a financial hit. Mike's attitude reduced my stress and my worry because he had perspective.

Perspective means having a true understanding of the relative importance of things. In other words, taking a moment to think about the situation in relation to the big issues of life and coming to the conclusion that "It's no big deal."

In Spencer Johnson's small book titled, "Peaks and Valleys," he points out that a valley in life describes those times in life when you long for what is missing. You've lost your job. You've lost a relationship. You've lost your dignity, self-worth or worse, your purpose in life. You are in a valley.

Johnson goes on to say that one way to get out of the 'valleys' in life is to make reality your friend. In other words, look at your situation and ask yourself these questions:

"Is it really as bad as it seems?"
"Is my judgment being clouded by my emotions?"

Most of the time, the answer to that first question is 'no' and the last question, 'yes'.

Defiance

It reminds me of Jesus' preaching on the hills north of the Sea of Galilee. He sees thousands of local people, struggling to get by in life and stressed under the burden of simply providing for their families. In the words of the sermon on the mount, Jesus says,

"Therefore I tell you, do not worry about your life, what you will eat or drink; or about your body, what you will wear. Is not life more than food, and the body more than clothes? Look at the birds of the air; they do not sow or reap or store away in barns, and yet your heavenly Father feeds them. Are you not much more valuable than they? Can anyone of you by worrying add a single hour to your life?"

- Matthew 6:25-27

In times of pain and difficulty, our vision becomes myopic. We can only see the problem and struggle to see any solution. But throughout scripture, God tells us to practice seeing every situation in light of what really matters in life. Remember that no matter how simple or complex the struggle, God won't give you more than you can handle and when He does, He supplies what you need.

A God-given perspective melts away bitterness, envy or guilt. A Spirit-filled attitude can make even the most ornery, defiant person calm and enthusiastic about their future purpose. Change can be scary but it can also be exciting because it gives us an opportunity to focus upward, to know God's love, and to humbly trust that God is God, we are not, and that He still knows what He's doing in your life.

For some of you, you have not released the reins in your life and trusted the LORD. God may be asking you right now to give up the control, to give up trying to run the universe, let alone your life – that's His job. Don't hang on to fear that keeps you from the life God want's you to enjoy.

I read about a guy who, after digging up what appeared to be an unexploded WWI bomb, held on to it for 4 hours. He was afraid that letting go would detonate the device.

While holding the bomb, the terrified 40-year-old from Norfolk, England, called an emergency operator on his mobile phone. He even used the call to issue his last words for his family. "The woman police operator kept saying it would be okay," said the man, "but I kept saying to her, 'You're not the one holding the bomb.'"

First responders rushed to the work-yard in eastern England, and army bomb disposal experts finally arrived. But the drama came to an abrupt end when the "bomb" was identified. It was part of the hydraulic suspension system from a Citroen, a popular European car.

I don't think I need to explain the application to your life because it's so simple and so obvious -- when you worry, you turn small pieces of junk into huge piles of explosives. Worrying does nothing for you.

God provides what you need. Again ...

"Therefore I tell you, do not worry about your life, what you will eat or drink; or about your body, what you will wear. Is not life more important than food, and the body more important than clothes? Look at the birds of the air; they do not sow or reap or store

away in barns, and yet your heavenly Father feeds them. Are you not much more valuable than they? Who of you by worrying can add a single hour to his life?"

- Matthew 6:25-27

Let go.
It's not a bomb.
And you're going to be okay!

6

LONELINESS

LONELINESS

Look for Signs of God's Presence

"Even though I walk through the valley of the shadow of death, I will fear no evil, for you are with me"
- Psalm 23:4

"To be awake is to be alive." -- Henry David Thoreau

Have you ever been alone? I mean, really alone? I'm not talking about the ugly feeling of loneliness that causes the deep slippage into the darkness of depression. But rather, the feeling that no one understands, no one feels the deep gnaw of your hurt, and no one is willing to go the distance with you. You may be hoping for someone with whom you could share the pain. But there is no one. You are alone.

The metal is not alone in the crucible. If I tried to melt a gold necklace by itself, the quality of the gold would diminish, making it less valuable for use again. For the metal to be melted-transformed-refined, the refiner adds pure white powder mix called "flux." (The main ingredients are Borax and Soda Ash -- for those of you who want to know). The purpose of the flux is two-fold. First, it is to help separate out the impurities in the metal and second, to absorb those impurities as if they were it's own. The flux gives up its holy white appearance and takes on the ugliness of the metal's faults.

Experts tell us that 60 million people in America would describe themselves as lonely. This is not a good statistic. Even from the beginning of creation, God said,

"It is not good for man to be alone."
- *Genesis 2:18*

It is interesting that even the Hebrew transliteration (sounding out of a word) for the word "alone" is "bad." In other words, if you were speaking Hebrew and wanted to say the word "alone," you would say the English word "bad." God knew what He was saying. Again, it is bad for people to be alone. In our country, however, many people feel like they are.

Luis Palau, an evangelist, wanted to speak on subjects that most reflected what was on the minds of people. At one of his crusades, he asked the people in his audience to indicate the subject on which they would most like him to speak. Many different themes were suggested: prayer, fasting, marriage etc. However, the majority requested him to speak on the subject of loneliness.

The people picked out the subject that is most pervasive in our society today, loneliness. Even with FaceBook and

Twitter's ability to connect people online, people's sense of loneliness is increasing.

This brings up a needed comparison. There is a difference between being alone and feeling lonely. Last spring, I went to see the sites in Old City, Jerusalem. If you've been there, you know what a life-changing adventure it can be. We stayed in hostels, graced the touristy sites and spent time processing the life of Jesus when He walked the city streets. One of the days, our group decided to go back and spend more time at the Church of the Holy Sepulcher. Having been there before, I decided to strike out on my own and explore some of the back alleyways of this historic city.

Most of the streets are, at best, 15 feet wide with small, hundred-year old shops that dot every nook. There are few cars and tons of people. It didn't take long for me to realize I had no idea where I was. I knew that eventually, I'd recognize a building, storefront or restaurant, but at the time, I was dithering. *Maybe it's this way. Or maybe I should take a left and the next alley.* I was lost.

Stumbling around a corner, I found myself on a larger street and in the middle of an even larger crowd. The group was so densely packed that I had no option but to walk in the same way direction. Turning to the guy uncomfortably close to me, I asked if he knew where my hostel was. He looked at me funny and simply said, "Polska." Yes, I was in the middle of a Christian pilgrimage group from Poland. No English, just Polish. I couldn't get out. I couldn't communicate. I knew no one and no one knew me. I was a disconnected human in the sea of a connected human group being moved along by the ebb and flow of people whose language was spoken through puckered lips.

At that moment, in the middle of hundreds, I was lonely. That's the funny thing about loneliness. It doesn't have to do with people proximity. It has everything to do with people connection. Pain and grief cause disconnection which is fuel for the fires of loneliness.

As a Pastor, I have counseled several families that had lost children. Whether infant or older adult, the strain on the family relationships takes it's toll. Some of the families I knew have exploded. Couples I knew are no longer together. It's the sad reality of such a traumatic experience.

Some studies point out that the divorce rate among marrieds who had lost a child was as high as 82%. The reason is simple. As a natural response, both spouses circle their individual wagons to heal from the loss. Experts say this is what needs to happen but if no emotional connection is made with the other spouse during that time, it leads to loneliness, bitterness, blame, and eventually separation.

If you've journeyed this far in the book, you've read the story of our daughter's sudden and tragic death. Kellie and I could have landed on the pages of the experts' study. We understand the sadness and statistics. However, the night our daughter Makenzie was killed, we looked each other, eye to eye, and made the verbal agreement that no matter how hard the next few days, months and years were, we were not going to become another number in the studies. We decided to do what it takes for ourselves, our families and our witness of God's sustaining power. It's been difficult, but God has honored our commitment and is strengthening our marriage even today!

Along with taking a stand for our marriage, the tragedy forced me to devour scripture like I've never read it in the past. The events before and after her welcome into heaven on June 3, 2009, catapulted me into a constant study of how God works and comforts during the journey of grief. One of the most helpful chapters that danced off the pages of my well-marked Bible was Psalm 77. Simply put, the Psalm is a description of the Christian's experience with God in the middle of hardship. The Message Paraphrase says,

"I yell out to my God, I yell with all my might, I yell at the top of my lungs. He listens. I found myself in trouble and went looking for my Lord; my life was an open wound that wouldn't heal.

When friends said, 'Everything will turn out all right,' I didn't believe a word they said. I remember God and shake my head. I bow my head then wring my hands. I'm awake all night—not a wink of sleep; I can't even say what's bothering me. I go over the days one by one, I ponder the years gone by. I strum my lute[ix] all through the night, wondering how to get my life together."

- Psalm 77:1-6 (MSG)

Have you ever felt like that? That you just wanted to scream because the intensity of your situation burned like the heat of a furnace? You couldn't sleep. Friends tried to say well-meaning cliques but none of it helped. This is pain and this is the experience of many.

The Psalmist moves from describing how he feels about his situation to how he feels about God.

"Will the Lord walk off and leave us for good? Will he never smile again? Is his love worn threadbare? Has his salvation promise burned out? Has God forgotten his manners? Has He angrily stalked off and left us?
"'Just my luck,' I said. 'The High God goes out of business just the moment I need Him.'"
- Psalm 77:7-9 (MSG)

The Psalmist had my attention. It was as if his words were written about my life. When I read this, I was asking myself, "How do I deal with this pain? How can I ever worship and trust God again? How can I, as a Pastor, say that He loves me when it seems like He doesn't?"

For many, they stop reading the Psalm. They stop trusting God. They stop seeing His goodness. They believe that God has put a FOR SALE sign in the window of His mercy and moved to the suburbs. Struggle and tragedy seem to silence God's voice. But the next verse changes everything. It gives a "how to" perspective on dealing with grief. The King James Version says it best:

"And I said, 'This is my infirmity: but I will remember the years of the right hand of the most High.'"
- Psalm 77:10

How do you begin to deal with the loneliness caused by grief and pain? First, you affirm the reality of your situation[x] and then you become aware of how God has worked in your life in the past. You don't look at the present struggles, you think about the past successes. The God-given victories over obstacles. The God-ordained comfort during painful situations. The God-spoken peace that came through scripture or a friend in the midst of a depressing time of your life. You deal with present loneliness by being aware of His past goodness[xi]. But that doesn't mean He isn't working in your present situation. It doesn't mean that He'll be involved during one chapter of your life and not the others.

The last verse of The Message Paraphrase of Psalm 77 says:

"<u>Hidden</u> in the hands of Moses and Aaron, You led your people like a flock of sheep."
- *Psalm 77:20*

In many things, in many ways, while God seems absent or out of business during your current circumstance, the reality is that He is right there in the middle of it! You may feel like you're on your own but God promises never to leave you -- especially when life is heating up! Psalm 34:18 says that He is near the brokenhearted. Psalm 23:4 says that when you feel like you are in the deepest darkness and that no one is there with you, that you don't have to worry. Why? Because God is with you. Leading. Guiding. Having everything under control. Even in the bleakest of circumstances.

Loneliness

Struggle and adversity seems to quiet the voice of God but realize that we have a Savior who not only walked into the furnace of sin for us but took on our impurities to make us holy.

You are not alone. Friends may not be holding your hand. Family may not come around, but God is in the crucible with you. He has a purpose for your pain. And it is good.

When I was teaching 8th-grade religion at Lutheran South Academy in Houston, I noticed that one of my students was overly attentive when covering the topic of God's Power and Presence. Later, she wrote me about her crucible experience and how God changed her life.

"I am a Long-Term Cancer Survivor. I was diagnosed with Leukemia when I was three and went through a long process of chemotherapy for two and a half years. During that whole time, I had absolutely no idea why it was happening to me! I had always heard Cancer as being a giant monster that no one wanted to face, but then, for some reason, God picked ME to face that challenge. I didn't actually become a devoted Christian until I came to Lutheran South in the sixth grade. From then on I've realized that God put me up to that challenge because He knew that I would beat it with His help! I've also realized that what has happened to me makes me different in an awesome way. From a first-person perspective, I have seen God do a miracle on me. Now, anytime I face any sort of trial, I just take a look back, notice what God has

done and remember to 'Be Still and Know that He is God'" -- Abbey

Abby has perspective. Abby has awareness. Abby has an understanding that God is always with her and always has been, even when life isn't comfortable.

I recently preached a message on the difference between being comfortable and being comforted. I pulled a sofa on stage and sat very comfortably on one side with my arm stretched out on the back and legs crossed. I spoke about how it's one thing to be comfortable and quite another to be comforted and that there is a tension between these two words -- comfortable and comforted.

In our world and our society, we strive after the comfortable. In every way possible we buy things, store things, do things that feed that desire to be comfortable. And that desire for being comfortable drives people for more and more. Someone once said that *being comfortable* is that stealthy thing that enters the house a guest, and then becomes a host, and then a master.

If you've lived any time of years, you know life doesn't work in the way of comfort. There are experiences right around the corner that toss us off the couch of comfort. There are times when life is hard and when the consequences of our sin make us hurt. However, God allows pain in our life for a reason, for a purpose. Accompanied by those times of deep hurt, He lovingly provides deep comfort. Through His Word, through our experience of prayer, and through other people, the peace and comfort that surpasses our understanding carries us during life's most difficult transitions.

LONELINESS

A friend of mine's dad was lying in bed, waiting to die. It was a tough circumstance. He was young, energetic and was looking forward to so much. But cancer had riddled his body to a point of no return. My friend Erin and her husband gathered by his bedside along with other family memebers. It was Thanksgiving and they celebrated around him in the hospital. Soon, he would be in the arms of his Savior. Soon, he would be walking the streets of gold with no guilt, struggle or shame. He was battling his pain. The discomfort of dying was taking its toll. But in it all, he took solace in the Lord. Erin recalls his last moments ...

"As my dad was lying in bed the last days of his life, he would NOT let us cry at all because the best is yet to come. He wanted us to celebrate what God is doing. So we did! It was a really amazing experience. On Sunday, in the morning, he said 'Tonight, tonight, we will all worship Him'" We knew that he meant that we will all worship Jesus but my dad would be worshiping in heaven. Our family waited all day for that moment of death and then he passed at 8:13 pm (his birthday 8-13-56). His last words were 'We win, I'm free, I'm free.'"

You can be comforted and not comfortable. You can also be comfortable and not comforted. The greater of the two is to be able to be in any situation -- comfortable or not -- and receive peace in knowing that God is always with you. That's awareness. Being able to see that even in the midst of the pain of the broken relationship, shattered dreams, or wavering health, the Holy Spirit has not and will not leave you lonely.

There isn't anything that could pull us or Him from the bedside of our circumstance[xii]. Nothing! The weight of chaos, can't! The sting of brokenness can't! The darkness of depression can't! Nothing can! God is always present. We may not feel Him, we may not hear Him, but He is there and is guiding and directing the circumstances that we are experiencing. As Psalm 139 says,

> *"Where can I go from your Spirit? Where can I flee from your presence? If I go up to the heavens, you are there; if I make my bed in the depths, you are there. If I rise on the wings of the dawn, if I settle on the far side of the sea, even there your hand will guide me, your right hand will hold me fast."*
>
> *- Psalm 139:7-10*

LONELINESS

7

REFLECTION

Reflection

Choose to be Radiant

"And all of us have had that veil removed so that we can be mirrors that brightly reflect the glory of the Lord. And as the Spirit of the Lord works within us, we become more and more like him and reflect his glory even more."
- 2 Corinthians 3:18 (NLT)

"I adore wearing gems, but not because they are mine. You can't possess radiance, you can only admire it."
- Elizabeth Taylor

An average melt takes 22 minutes. Be it gold or silver, I can place the necklaces, bracelets, and rings into the Crucible and know that I need to check the melt after that time.

Lifting the lid of the Crucible, I'll take a carbon rod and stir the contents until I can see one thing: my reflection. It's not always easy to find. Many times, I'll stir among the "slag," squint through the smoke or jiggle the Crucible to get

Reflection

at it, but inevitably, there it will be; the shining metal reflecting back the image of its refiner.

Before becoming a refiner, I read in a book somewhere, (probably Max Lucado's *"On the Anvil"*), that is what happens to melted metal. But until I saw it with my own eye's, I could not comprehend this beautiful outcome of the Crucible process. (I wish you could see it as well).

Just seeing myself in the liquid metal showed that the melt was ready to be poured into a new mold. But the joy I find as a refiner looking into the metal is not in my reflection, but in the metal's radiance. Words only hint at the reality of its dazzle. The melt is pure (mostly); brilliant; waiting and wanting to be used in its new form, whatever that would be.

The Crucible has provided its protection, its form, it's focused heat. The Crucible has liquefied my defiance and burned off impurities. Things that would hold me back are now encased in the disposable slag. The Crucible has changed me into something new; something beautiful in God's eyes. And now, see God's reflection in me, I am ready to be used by my Savior Refiner.

So far, the process of turning pain into purpose has been bleak. Leading up to and experiencing pain and grief is never fun. It is hard. It is frustrating. It can turn your world upside down and sometimes, even creates a new normal.

Our immediate reaction to pain is to withdraw. Think of touching a hot surface. Your body's reactive state is pulling back to a place of safety. That is how it is with emotional pain or distress.

If the event is hurtful enough, we may even want to rewind the clock. We want to go back to the way it was, even if it was a struggle to being with. We do not want to proceed any further in the process of hurt because we are creatures of comfort and normalcy. However, this is an indication that we are focusing on the occurrence and not on who God is or what He can do through it.

After a year and a half, my wife's struggle was deep. The first year after Makenzie's death was novel (not in a good way) but into the second year, we were trying to figure out the "what now?" of our lives. Kellie exchanged an email conversation with a dear friend.

> ***From:*** *"Kellie Stocker"*
> ***Date:*** *December 3, 12:43 PM CST*
> ***To:*** *"Deborah Dalby"*
> *Hi Debbie,*
> *Today marks a year and a half since Makenzie's death. It's hard each day and I just miss her joy and always will. It's been a hard week to get into the Advent anticipation of Christ as we used to in years past but we know we need to for our son Nathan and daughter Maddie and because the Lord has life left for us to live.*
> *But, if I could just rewind...*
> *Love and miss you,*
> *Kellie*

REFLECTION

From: "Deborah Dalby"
Date: December 3, 2:17 PM CST
To: "Kellie Stocker"
Hi, Kellie.
How wonderful that God put me on your heart. What did you mean in your email, "If you could just rewind..." Then what? What would you really do? I found Isaiah 57:1 -- "The righteous perish, and no one ponders it in his heart; devout men are taken away, and no one understands that the righteous are taken away to be spared from evil." This doesn't mean that the rest of us are left because we're unrighteous or not devout. But it has given me comfort that there are so many pains that Makenzie has now been spared. It's true that she has also missed out on many human joys and we miss out on sharing those with her, but she has also been spared from whatever things Satan would have flung at her.

If you had the chance to prevent the accident, would you? Would you take away this catalyst that has brought several young people to repentance and faith, and touched so many more and made their hearts more open to God? I know you want to, but if you were really given that opportunity, could you look Jesus in the face and do it?

I don't mean that as a lecture, it's just that her life and death has brought new and renewed purpose to so many because she reflected her Savior. There are so many who don't know Him and will be changed by hearing your testimony.
Love to you as well,
Debbie

Pain hurts. Our natural reaction is to want desperately to go back to a time before the event that caused it. We want to take another road, go a different way, experience a better path. However, it may be that suffering is the only way to growth. As much as we'd like to rewind the event of Makenzie's death, we are also grateful for what we've seen happen in and through us. You may be new on the journey. You may be or will be experiencing something that completely shakes your world. If you are a newbie, my caution to you is not to jump right into the "God has a better plan" thinking. Don't miss the healing that comes in the grieving.

Make a note that this conversation happened well after the tragic event that caused our pain. One of the worst things people can say immediately after a difficult situation to someone is, "God's got a plan." We heard this many times after our life-change and it came from the void of not knowing what to say. Sure, the sentiment is true, but these misplaced words can cause people young or weak in faith to turn against God, not toward him.

A deep experience of pain can change the way you radiate. The Bible says,

Reflection

"Pure gold put in the fire comes out of it proved pure; genuine faith put through this suffering comes out proved genuine. When Jesus wraps this all up, it's your faith, not your gold, that God will have on display as evidence of His victory."

- 1 Peter 1:7 (The Message Paraphrase)

Unless we go through pain, we don't know what our faith really looks like. Not the faith that God gave that saved you. That's a done deal in Christ. The faith that is proved pure is the faith that trusts God, even when He seems untrustworthy. It is a faith that holds onto His promises even when tragedy tempts you to let go. It is a faith that reflects the calm strength of the face of God. I've heard it said that your true image bubbles to the surface under the boiling of stress. I believe this to be true simply from observing people.

Peace or Panic?

When I worked at a hotel during high school, there was a front desk manager who everyone said 'had a temper.' When I first met him, I thought he was kind, friendly and outgoing, not the person I was expecting. But when our front desk team had lines of people backing up and double booked hotel rooms, he would charge out from his office and -- in front of the guests -- rip into whoever was in his eyesight. A torrent of anger and ridicule spewed from the raging volcano set just under his persona. What he reflected about himself was his true colors. Angry. Bitter. Hot-tempered. His was a reflection at which no one wanted to look.

Contrast his outbursts to that of one of my co-workers at the front desk. Her name was Toni and she too was kind, friendly and outgoing. But her manner and reflection were much different. On one occasion, we had the Milwaukee Brewers baseball team staying at our hotel. Less than an hour before they arrived, we were notified they were not in the best of moods. For one, they had lost a pivotal game that afternoon and for another, the hotel at which they were originally booked, had messed up the dates, giving their rooms to a McDonnell Douglas sales convention. To add to the confusion, the players themselves were required to come to the front desk to check in and get room assignments.

They were not happy.

Late that night, their bus rolled up and 30 or so players shuffled into our neatly arranged lobby. It was instant pandemonium. As we began the check-in process, we found that certain players didn't want to be in the same room with others. Some wanted to be on a certain floor and still, others had special bed-size requests. Most of the players, while tired, were still cordial. A few were arrogant, loud and demanding. The latter were the ones who ended up in Toni's line. Toni didn't buckle. With a firm and gracious attitude, she met the rooming needs of the players, didn't raise her voice and most of them went away calmer than when they came in.

It was beautiful.

After the chaos simmered and the lobby cleared out, I asked Toni how she was able to stay relaxed with that ornery group of players. She smiled said, "I simply put my mind into their shoes and responded from my heart." There it was. Responding from the heart -- that's Reflection. What was *inside* Toni reflected onto the players and it was good.

The background story was that Toni was raised in an abusive family. From early on, she was told by her parents that she would never amount to anything because she had a learning disability. Her siblings and extended family were always fighting and she remembers making a conscious decision that she would use the verbal abuse to make her stronger inside rather than weaker. I don't remember if she was a Christ-follower or not, but her life's reflection was that of Divinity.

Everyone has bad days -- even weeks. There are times when I lose my cool or feel depressed. There are situations in which I don't act with integrity toward people with whom I struggle. Just because you have speed bumps like these doesn't mean your reflection is horrible. I saw Toni lose her cool with a few customers and I saw my manager be nice to a few as well. In order to test your current reflection and get a sneak peek at what's beneath the surface of your life, simply ask yourself:

What is my normal pattern of behavior? In other words, if you look back over the last 3-6 months, can you realistically say that you responded to most people and frustrations with a finesse or with fire?

How have I been feeling about my life? Everyone experiences times of struggle and disappointment. But if you can say that 80% of your outlook is positive, then your core is radiating the Holy Spirit's guidance in your life.

How do you think your friends would describe you? Going through life's trauma's reveals your true self. The people around you can notice slight changes in your behavior and reaction. Check with them for an objective assessment of how you've been responding to life.

Are you at peace this very moment? I'm not talking about a feeling but more so a subtle confidence. The peace that Jesus talks about is not a feeling-based peace but a God-based one. God says that you are the radiance of Himself.

In Him, we see a glimpse of the reflection and radiance of who we were originally created to be. Right from the beginning, God created humanity in His image[xiii]. Even though that image was tarnish by sin, the Lord is still working on and in us to recapture that image and make us radiant like His Son, Jesus. He is the one to whom we look to see the image that has been placed in us. The Bible says,

"(Jesus) is the image of the invisible God,"
- Col. 1:15

That means in our trials and pain, we can look at the life of Jesus to see how he handled the stress-filled, chaotic times. When pressure was on him, he gave it to his heavenly Father through prayer. When people were demanding his time, he would do what he could then retreat to a quiet place to recharge. In doing so, Jesus radiated God's divinity.

Reflection

The problem many of us face is that we look at ourselves in the mirror and don't like what looks back. We know our secrets, our thoughts, our hidden actions. We know what we've done and who we've hurt. We see ourselves as the useless slag that forms during a melting time and not the radiant metal underneath.

It reminds me of one of the molds into which I'd pour lower grade gold. It was the messiest of them all -- the cone mold. Of all of the molds, this one yielded the most potential for, what is called, "spitting." When the molten metal is ready to be poured, the receiving mold needs to be at a warm enough temperature to keep the metal from reacting violently to the difference in temperature. If I didn't warm up the mold, most likely the pour would spit out little drops of metal; landing on and burning holes in the protective jacket. Sometimes, the spitting drops would land on the exposed skin on my wrists, in between my glove and coat.

All refiners have scars and even as I write this I'm looking at the scars on my wrists. It reminds me of my Savior Refiner who bore scars to save useless people and "refine" them into a new and purpose-filled life. But that's another book.

The cone mold is especially conducive to spitting because as I warm it up, the top of the cone is the farthest away from the warmer, making it the coolest part of the form. I pour -- it spits. I keep pouring -- it keeps spitting until the total pour is done and the ugly, black slag forms and covers the beautiful gold. But what is happening under the crust is glorious. The gold is cooling and forming and releasing the remaining impurities into the slag. When cooled, I chip away the top and reveal the radiant shine of the metal.

Life is exactly the same. The pressures of dealing with pain and juggling the new normal can make our life messy. At times, people, situations, and emotions "spit" at us and leave scars. But your Savior Refiner knows that through this process, He will make you radiant! James 1:2 says,

"Consider it a sheer gift, friends, when tests and challenges come at you from all sides. You know that under pressure, your faith-life is forced into the open and shows its true colors."
- James 1:2 (The Message Paraphrase)

You may have entered the crucible broken and useless -- worthy only to be thrown out. But God rescued you through that violent process. He let His Son die the death of a criminal for you. Jesus became worthless slag, you became precious gold. As a result, you are being transformed into the very image of Christ Himself. The Bible says,

"Where the Spirit of God is, we are free. All of us! Nothing between us and God, our faces shining with the brightness of his face. And so we are transfigured much like the Messiah, our lives gradually becoming brighter and more beautiful as God enters our lives and we become like him."
- 2 Corinthians 3:18 (The Message Paraphrase)

8

TIMING

TIMING

Wait for His Unfolding Purpose

"For I know the thoughts that I think toward you, saith the LORD, thoughts of peace, and not of evil, to give you an expected end." -- Jeremiah 29:11 (KJV)

"We never truly 'arrive' at the destination called 'healed.' We will always carry the scars of this life's thuggery.'"
- Kellie Stocker

As a refiner, I can make a hefty mess of the newly melted metal. Now liquid, the soup is poured out from the Crucible and into a preselected mold to cool. The timing of this move is critical. If I empty this 'new creation' too soon, the slag and metal could be malformed and be of sub-quality for use. If I allow the mass to stay in the Crucible too long, it will get stuck; never wanting to leave the comfort of its coffin-shaped bed.

When my Savior Refiner dropped me in the Crucible on June 3rd, all I could do was trust that this inferno was merely a flicker to Him. When my Savior Refiner allowed

TIMING

me to experience the heat of grief and the singe of loss, all I could do was watch my pride and self-reliance melt away. And now that my Savior Refiner has poured me into a new mold, all I can do is rely on His plan and purpose. He will either keep me in the mold to 'cool' or pop me out to be used. Either way, it will be in His perfect timing.

We moved into a home a few blocks from one of its entrances. I remember seeing it for the first time. Lush open landscape. Wide expanses that pushed out the tree lines. Slow rolling hills cut in half by a winding path just large enough for a golf cart.

Yes, it was a golf course[xiv]. Opened in the 1960's, it used to be the center-point of the then, new neighborhood. Now, however, there were no players on the course. There were no caddies or foursomes. No hollers or beer-carts buzzing around the holes. The hole markers were still there. Big, stone features listed the number, distance to the pin and terrain. Like old gravestones, many had been tipped over, some vandalized. Sadly, this course, in the middle of a busy neighborhood, sat empty and unused.

Kellie and I would take walks together on it's twisting paths, finding old golf balls that had been long forgotten by their hack-player owners. Each time I was on that abandon course, I'd think, *how sad that such a beautiful expanse is not being used for its original purpose.*

I know things change. With a little research, I found out that the course had been sold, fell into disrepair and is now in the hands of the courts, -- fighting over deed restrictions. Again, sad.

Everything has a time and a purpose. Yesterday's victories become today's memories. Today's grief becomes tomorrow's motivation. Things die. Others flourish. That's just the way God set up the ebb and flow of life. As it says in the familiar passage of Ecclesiastes,

> *"There is a time for everything, and a season for every activity under the heavens: a time to be born and a time to die, a time to plant and a time to uproot, a time to kill and a time to heal, a time to tear down and a time to build, a time to weep and a time to laugh, a time to mourn and a time to dance, a time to scatter stones and a time to gather them, a time to embrace and a time to refrain from embracing, a time to search and a time to give up, a time to keep and a time to throw away, a time to tear and a time to mend, a time to be silent and a time to speak, a time to love and a time to hate, a time for war and a time for peace."*
>
> *Ecclesiastes 3:1-8*

At this point, you may still be wondering, "What is the purpose for my pain? Why did this happen to me? Will I ever get over this?" Many of these natural questions we ask describe the human quest for meaning in life. In our humanness, we expect God to answer them and that in His answers, there is satisfaction. There may be, but God is not obligated to answer any of our questions. In His love and by His watch, He gives us what we need to make it through the next moment, minute and day. His daily bread is not just physical needs, but also emotional and spiritual as well.

In the process of turning pain into purpose, there is the crucial thread of timing. It runs from beginning to end. There was a reason that at just the exact time, you experienced the pain of loss, struggle or frustration. There was a timing that happened as you fought against your experience. The clock ticked true when you began to sense that everything was going to be all right. It's God's timing and the best we can do is roll with it.

I had experienced loss and pain in my life in the past and had forced myself to push too fast through the grief process. In doing so, I ended up prolonging my healing process rather than turning it into purpose. When my daughter was killed, I knew that I needed to let the process of refining work in me. I knew that if I listened to the well-meaning -- but badly timed -- comments that told me "God has a plan," "She's in a better place," etc, that I'd circumvent the healing process and ruin its work in me.

The issue of allowing the Refiner to determine the timeline is an important one. However, you may respond to His timing in two different ways:

1. You might want to fight the Lord's encouragement to move on.

You may want to stay in bed all day, all the time. Actually, it's ok to have those recovery days. I called them my Makenzie Moments and I still have them. But you need help if, after a year, you are consistently finding yourself spending one or two days a week hiding under the covers. You are not allowing the Refiner to pour His strength into your weakness. You are not trusting that God is holding your hand as you step out into the world and carry the burden of your hurt.

When I was refining metal, there were times when the melt refused to come out of the mold. When that happened, I'd have to turn the mold over and bang it hard with a sledge hammer. Not fun. If it really stayed stuck, I'd grab a jackhammer and have to subject the stubborn gold bar to a more brutal process of chipping at it. This resulted in the loss of some of it's value. Metaphorically, *you do not want to be jack-hammered by God!*

So how do you know when it's time to move on? As vague as this sounds, you don't. The grieving process involves many factors: the depth of loss, the situation around the pain, your environment etc. The greatest unknown is you. Every person is different. Every person's reaction and restoration time varies and the process of grief does not go step by step. It is cyclical, meaning, one day you may feel great, the next you may be crying at the drop of a hat.   The best answer to "when is the right time" is -- you'll know.

Sorry. It's not an easy answer but it's the truth. The Holy Spirit will guide you forward. He'll impress on your heart or bring someone into your life that encourages a next step. I can hear some of you say, "It's been years and I still feel so stuck." Truthfully, the *feelings* of pain change over time but the ache will always be there. Examine those times when you feel stuck. What is happening in your life? How high is your stress level? Are you using your grief as an excuse not to try something new?

2. You might want to move past your pain too quickly, thinking that you are strong enough to handle it.

The goal of turning pain into purpose is not to get better, faster. If the goal were to get better, what happens when you don't reaching that goal on your timeline, if ever? That creates a gap between your expectations of being ok and the reality that you may not be. The larger the gap, the deeper the pain.

A few years ago, I was speaking at a conference, sharing our story about turning pain into purpose. After the session, I met a women who came to me in tears. She had lost a baby to SIDS[xv]. As she spoke, I could hear, see and "feel" the internal battle through which she was journeying. Every phrase of despair and grief was coupled with a phrase of Christian platitude. She talked about how empty and lost she feels but how God has a purpose. Through her tears, she spoke of the pain with which she's been dealing but how she knows "all things will work out." Honestly, I felt really sad for her. Sad for her loss, but more so for the struggle to keep strong, waged on the battlefield of her sanity. Her expectation of her strength and the reality of her weakness created a huge gap of pain.

I asked her, "How long has it been since your baby died?" With her emotionality, I was expecting the answer *a few months*.

She replied, "Thirteen years ago."

I didn't know what to say. For more than a decade, this poor woman tried to talk herself into believing that she was okay, strong enough to handle the emotional road of grief. In my opinion and based on our conversations, I'll bet that she never allowed herself to truly grieve. I'll bet that someone, maybe herself, told her that she needed to buck up and that it was going to be ok. That advice can come but my guess is that, for her, it came too quickly.

In God's perfect timing, He'll pull you out of the crucible mold. The mold has shaped you. The mold has made it's imprint on you. The mold's divots and cracks are now yours. Like the pillow lines on your cheek in the morning, the indentations of what you've been through are now yours. Don't rush the process. Don't push for healing. Let the hurt do it's work because the Crucible and mold are simply tools for something greater.

There's still more refining to do.

As I mentioned in the first chapter, the grieving process is not linear. You do not start at point A, progress to point B and on to the end. You never finish grieving. There are times when, out of nowhere, tears push to the surface and the flood gates open. You feel like you're back at step one. My wife, Kellie, said something that hit me regarding this. She said,

> *"We never truly 'arrive' at the destination called 'healed'. We will always carry the scars of this life's thuggery."*

It reminds me, once again, of the illustration of the process of the metal. Battled and bruised, the metal is still not done. Once it is flipped out of the mold, it is subjected to more abuse. Since there are still some residues of the slag on the gold bar, they need to be removed through chipping and buffing. Hard and heavy hammer hits chip away at the stubborn impurities that hold fast to the metal. Violent and fast wire brushing pulls out and smooths the surface of the bar. Unless this brutal process of removing the filth is done, the metal still remains useless. Like it says in Proverbs,

"Remove impurities from the silver and the silversmith can craft a fine chalice."
- Proverbs 25:4-5 (The Message Paraphrase)

Nice sentiment and very true. But that process of "removing impurities" is difficult. It's long. And it is a constant process.

My friend Trish's story is a unique and brave one. In August of 1995, Trish's sister and her family were driving their van out of town for a weekend away. With their boat in tow, Dad, Mom and their three children couldn't wait to meet up with their friends for some fun and recreation. But the weekend was about to unfold in a totally new way.

Another driver had borrowed a friend's car to drive to Blythe, California. The tires on his car were practically bald and he was speeding quite excessively. One of the tires blew and he veered into the family's van. The van and boat jackknifed, causing the van to roll several times. Trish's sister and husband were both killed, leaving behind three children, two of which were not expected to live through the night. God miraculously healed these children and Trish and her husband moved to California to raise the three, now parentless children. Trish writes:

"I know I have not lost a child, but having raised three children who each lost a parent, I understand how grieving takes place over and over again, with each special event, each wedding, each birth, each you name it. It has been many years since the accident but I could tell you the details as if it were yesterday. When someone close to you dies at such a young age, it impacts the rest of your life.
However, God certainly had a plan though we did not know what it was. For example, my husband who was a pastor, ended up taking a part time job in children's ministry, a job my sister was to start just a few short days after the car accident.

Over the years, we have seen God's hand in so many things. When my nephew needed additional help, we found a boy's ranch program in the state of Washington, just a few hours from where my husband was assigned his first pastorate. We never would have considered this program had we not been familiar with the area due to those first few years in the ministry.

Shortly after we moved to Pennsylvania, the sister of a young couple in our church died, and suddenly they became guardians to their nieces and nephew…..we walked beside this couple as we knew exactly what they were going through and would go through, since we had lived it.

Many times over the years, we have sat in the hospital with others, understanding their pain and fears….because we had walked the very road that they were walking. God had a plan and used it in our ministry."

I cannot imagine the courage it took for Trish and her family not only to deal with the loss of Trish's sister and her husband, but then to make the decision to raise the three children who were on the verge of death's door. There were many unknown's for them including Trish's husband giving up his public ministry to move across the country and start a new life. Trish's new role as a mom and caretaker. It hasn't been easy but as they have learned to lean on God, they now can see how He has used the fires of loss to forge them into a resource for others.

How do you know when God is moving you from stage to stage? You know when you know.

You Know When You Know

There's a maturity that comes with tragedy, a growing that takes place in the heart, mind and soul of a person who's lost something or someone significant. The initial shock places you into the book of grief and the only way out is by turning the pages. But as you watch the story of your life change, you'll come to realize that this challenge, this trial, this test produces maturity. James 1 says,

> *"... the testing of your faith produces perseverance. Let perseverance finish its work so that you may be mature and complete, not lacking anything."*
> - *James 1:4*

In this verse, James is telling us not to rush the process. He is saying that in order to grow and mature, you have to take on the mentality of a passenger rather than a driver. You have to *"let perseverance finish it's work"* or else you'll never grow past the infancy stage of dealing with your loss.

Remember the woman a few pages back who, after 13 years, couldn't handle her life's loss? She never *let* the struggle work itself out. Maturity never had a chance.

There will come a time when you know that there has been progress. You may not *feel* it, but you simply know it. For me, it was when I could reach out and encourage others intentionally again. When I was placed at Concordia University in St. Paul, MN as the Campus Chaplain and I could have a conversation with college-aged students about their lives without thinking about how it affected mine, that is when I knew that I was being "plopped" out of the mold and maturity was beginning to shine.

To summarize, you will not know when God is moving you from stage to stage, at least not when it's happening. There will be glimpses of His timing in your attitudes and feelings. There will be moments of victory and strength.

There will be signs of maturity as your new normal takes hold but remember -- DO NOT FORCE HIS TIMING!

Ultimately, God does have a purpose for you. Every experience, every situation, every reaction is woven into His purpose that plays out in your life.

A friend of mine once said, "Don't go looking for purpose. Eventually, *it* will find *you*." I really like that statement because who would've known that God would use the experiences of your past to bring you to where you are today. Who could've guessed that God would use the choice you made a dozen years ago to put you in a perfect position to help make life better for someone else. That's purpose, and it is orchestrated, written, woven and designed by the Lord who died so the world could live.

God's timing is His, not yours. So weep when you want to weep. Call in sick when you're emotionally sick. Laugh when you want to laugh. It's ok. God is the one designing and revealing His purpose in and through your life. All you need to do is trust Him.

9

AND NOW ...

And Now

A Word of Encouragement

There is a pine tree that is indigenous in the Rocky Mountains that has an interesting character trait. These scraggly and thin-barked trees -- called Lodgepole Pine Tree -- need exposure to high temperatures in order for them to release their seeds. While they also can spread their seed at the maturity of their pine cones, most often it takes forest fires to launch their life giving seeds.

As I reflect on the years before and since Makenzie's death, I realize that in many ways, my life is like this silly little tree -- going through life, always thinking about the future, avoiding conflict or pain, and not realizing that struggle is the premier way in which God grows me and helps others through me. I know that the Lord has used my life to help others. It is only now, after the forest fire of my daughter's death, that I truly feel that His greatest work is ahead.

As I write this, I am transitioning back into a congregation as a Pastor, a position that I thought would never be given to me again. And I carry with me a refining moment that I know He'll use.

And Now

    I do not know for sure what's ahead -- none of us does. I do not know what other fires or refining the Lord has for me, but whatever it is, I know that He will guide me through the Crucible experience.

It will hurt.
              It won't be all fun.
                              That's how this life goes.

    But I do know that no matter how difficult the trial, He is greater still. He has given us His word as the Master Refiner to meet us where we are and take us to where He wants us to be. He is the one who always holds the tongs of control, even as we are being lowered into the fiery furnace of pain.

    I pray that these writings have encouraged you. My goal is simply to share my experience and in doing so, help you realize that He is the source of strength from which we draw. He is the purifier of all things. And as I've written before, there is nothing that you experience that doesn't first filter through the fingers of the Lord.

    So in your pain, turn to Him. In your grief and sorrow, find comfort in Him. And when you feel like you will never be the same, remember that you are right. You won't ever be the same. You'll be so much better.

"Consider it pure joy, my brothers and sisters, whenever you face trials of many kinds, because you know that the testing of your faith produces perseverance. Let perseverance finish its work so that you may be mature and complete, not lacking anything."
- *James 1:2-4*

AND NOW

REFINED

Turning Pain Into Purpose

Discussion Guide

Discussion Guide

Chapter One -- Our Story
"Is this Really Happening?"

Life Reflection: What is your Savior, Refiner doing in your life right now that is leading you from pain to purpose?

1. In most ways, our lives are good. Describe a time (maybe it's now) that you can honestly say that your life was good. What does that time look like?

2. There are times when we face "trials of many kinds." The Bible describes a trial as a struggle, a temptation or a testing of faith. Tell of a time (again, maybe it's now) that you have faced trials in your life. What does that time look like?

3. How did you get through that trial?

4. The more significant the struggle is, the more the process of healing affects you. What changes have you seen in your life as a result of journeying through the healing process?

5. How has your experience impacted other people?

6. Who can you invite on your life's journey of discovering purpose?

Chapter Two -- Illumination
"Change Your Attitude"

LIFE REFLECTION: What is your Savior, Refiner doing in your life right now that is leading you from pain to purpose?

1. The Dictionary defines the word "Attitude" as *the way a person views something or tends to behave towards it, often in an evaluative way*[xvi]. If you were to use a word or two to describe your attitude right now, what would that be?

2. If people around you (family, friends, co-workers) were to describe your overall attitude, what do you think they would say?

Discussion Guide

3. How has Attitude helped you in your past experience? How has it held you back?

4. Think back to a recent frustration or bad circumstance in which your attitude was not good. How do you think the outcome would have changed if your attitude was positive?

5. James 1:2 (NLT) says, "Dear brothers and sisters, whenever trouble comes your way, let it be an opportunity for joy!" In what ways do you think God helps us see our troubles as an opportunity for joy?

6. How can you live in a Godly attitude today?

Chapter Three -- Heating
"Prepare for the Journey"

Life Reflection: What is your Savior, Refiner doing in your life right now that is leading you from pain to purpose?

1. When hardships come our way, the natural reaction is to point the finger of blame at someone else. Sometimes it's justified. Other times, it's not. Describe a time when a trial you experienced was the result of someone else's misconduct or error.

2. Describe a time when a trial was the result of your own misconduct or error?

3. Respond to the statement, "God allows or causes hardships in our lives."

4. How has blaming God, or rather, acknowledging His control helped you in life.

5. How has it caused a heartache, if at all?

6. In John 16:33, Jesus says, "I have told you these things, so that in me you may have peace. In this world, you will have trouble. But take heart! I have overcome the world." How does this statement help prepare and sustain you on life's journey?

DISCUSSION GUIDE

CHAPTER FOUR -- PROTECTION
"Trust His Strength"

LIFE REFLECTION: What is your Savior, Refiner doing in your life right now that is leading you from pain to purpose?

1. Jonah 1:7 (NLT) says, "Now the Lord had arranged for a great fish to swallow Jonah. And Jonah was inside the fish for three days and three nights." If you were Jonah in the belly of the fish, what would you be thinking about how your situation was going to turn out?

2. What is your reaction to Robin's story of Haley on page 42?

3. Have you ever experienced the feeling of total helplessness when hard circumstances have you struggling? Describe what that looked like.

4. Do you think that God is obligated to provide protection for His people? Why or why not?

5. A common phrase in many Christians language is "Trust in His Strength." What are some ways in which you can trust Him?

Chapter Five -- Defiance
"Surrender to the Refiner"

Life Reflection: What is your Savior, Refiner doing in your life right now that is leading you from pain to purpose?

1. To be defiant means to be boldly resisting someone or something. When can this type of defiance be good? When can it be bad?

2. How would you describe a person that is defiant? What is it like to be around them?

3. Has there ever been a time when you've been defiant against God? What did that look like? What was the outcome?

4. What are some areas of your life in which you tend to be defiant against God and/or others? Is this a good thing?

5. When can surrendering in life be considered bad? When is it good?

6. In Matthew 26:39, Jesus prays that His will be surrender to God's. The bible implies that we should lead that kind of surrendered life as well? Describe what that may look like for you?

CHAPTER SIX -- LONELINESS
"Look for Signs of God's Presence"

LIFE REFLECTION: What is your Savior, Refiner doing in your life right now that is leading you from pain to purpose?

1. Read Psalm 23 out loud. What comfort does this Psalm give to you today?

2. How has Psalm 23 helped you in past trials or times of loneliness?

3. What are some areas in your life in which God has shown or can show His presence?

4. As is mentioned in this chapter, feelings of loneliness are not necessarily tied to being around people but more so describing the lack of emotional connection to others. Describe a time when you were in a crowd but still felt "lonely."

5. Do you feel emotionally connected to anyone currently? How could that help with the issue of 'loneliness'?

6. Who do you know that is seemingly lonely? How can you help?

Discussion Guide

Chapter Seven -- Reflection
"Choose to be Radiant"

Life Reflection: What is your Savior, Refiner doing in your life right now that is leading you from pain to purpose?

1. When our lives are hit with trials, we tend to withdraw and circle our wagons. Describe what that looks like in your life or in others.

2. What role do you think faith plays in the healing process?

3. 1 Peter 1:7 (MSG) says, "When Jesus wraps this all up, it's your faith, not your gold, that God will have on display as evidence of His victory." What do you think this means?

4. What are some qualities of Jesus that you could reflect in your own life when it comes to frustrating circumstances?

5. How can your reflection of faith be a help to someone else who is hurting in some way?

Chapter Eight -- Timing
"Wait for His Unfolding Purpose"

Life Reflection: What is your Savior, Refiner doing in your life right now that is leading you from pain to purpose?

1. The Bible is big on the topic of perseverance. Why do you think this is such a recurring theme to the Christ-follower?

2. Ecclesiastes 3:1-8 describes how, in life, we experience seasons of change. Think back over the past 5 years. What changes have you seen in your life? Which ones have been unexpected? (If you like, read Ecc. 3:1-8 and see which pairings of change have applied to you).

3. God's timing is perfect. Describe a time when you tried to rush through a situation and only later, realized you should have waited.

4. When have you felt the Holy Spirit's encouragement to move on but chose to 'stay in the mold'? What were the results?

5. In what ways has God shown purpose your life's story as a result of pain?

6. In what ways can you help others in their journey from pain to purpose?

CHAPTER NINE -- AND NOW
"A Word of Encouragement"

LIFE REFLECTION: What is your Savior, Refiner doing in your life right now that is leading you from pain to purpose?

1. Our life's refining process is never completed, this side of heaven. Do you feel this is good or bad? Explain?

2. God is always in control. He has done, is doing and will do great things through your life experiences -- good and bad. How may that change the way you live today?

3. How has this book's conversation helped you in your journey from pain to purpose?

4. What are some ways your story can help the people around you?

Discussion Guide

Other Books by The Author

Go To www.ToddStocker.com

"Becoming The Fulfilled Leader." As a successful businessman, Mike Worthington had it all. But now, after neglecting key personal and professional leadership principles, his company and his life were on the verge of collapse. That is until he met a simple janitor named Chuck. This is a story of two people who became unlikely friends and the conversations that produced fulfillment in the heart of a creative personality.

"Rosemont" Forty years ago, ROSEMONT was a thriving town until a mysterious murder. It is all turned around by a 11-year-old girl who encounters tragedy, forgiveness, and restoration. And it all begins in a town called ROSEMONT.

"BreakThrough Weight Loss: 5 Proven Ways To Get And Stay Healthy Today – Book or eBook." All of us would like to be in better shape and feel healthier. Todd lost 45 pounds using the methods he outlines in this book.

"Leading from the GUT: 3 Practice of Healthy Leaders – eBook." Leadership doesn't begin with what you do but with who you are. This eBook describes 3 practices that every leader should work on to become and healthy and long-lasting leader.

DISCUSSION GUIDE

"The Back to School Prayer Guide – eBook" Our kids are soon going back to school. This guide helps parents pray daily for them as they prepare to go back into the classroom.

"Dancing With God – First Year Thoughts on the Loss of My Daughter." All of us go through loss. This incredibly emotional book chronicles the year following an accident that killed Todd's oldest daughter. Join him on his journey of loss as he was comforted by the Lord in amazing and powerful ways.

"Manners Matter – 10 Table Manners Every Child Should Know." Eating a meal together as a family can be a wonderful opportunity for building closer relationships and having fun at the same time! Our book, "Manners Matter" can help begin conversations with your youngster about proper table manners and why they are important.

"Infinite Playlists – How to have Conversations, not Conflict, with your Child about Music." This is a handy guide to healthy conversation between parents and kids. Writing as both father and music-lover, Todd calls parents to recognize music as a gift from God so they can help their kids determine the emotional, physical, and spiritual influences of their song choices. He offers a balanced look at the difference between Christian and secular music and gives practical guidelines parents and kids can follow to choose appropriate music together.

For more, go to www.ChristianLeadersCoaching.com

NOTES

[i] After the accident, we recovered the flash card from the camera. If you'd like to see this and other pictures, they are in my previous book, "Dancing With God -- First Year Thoughts on the Loss of my Daughter."

[ii] Jeremiah 29:11 -- Makenzie's life verse.

[iii] You can read Chris's story at www.chrisgardnermedia.com/

[iv] The AMBER Alert website is www.amberalert.gov/

[v] Read Romans 5 for more on Hope.

[vi] It was preached at Grace Church, Houston Texas, www.grace.tv

[vii] Galatians 6:2 says "Carry each other's burdens, and in this way you will fulfill the law of Christ."

[viii] Read their furnace story in Daniel chapter 3.

[ix] A lute is a guitar-like instrument. Interestingly, Lute is also a clay-like substance that is used to coat the outside of a crucible.

DISCUSSION GUIDE

[x] Chapter 6 of this book talks more about this and other ideas about perspective.

[xi] The rest of Psalm 77 gives examples of what God has done.

[xii] Romans 8:38-39

[xiii] "So God created man in his own image, in the image of God created he him; male and female created He them." -- Genesis 1:27

[xiv] As of this writing, the Clear Lake City Golf Course is still viewable on google maps. Do a search on "Clear Lake City, TX," zoom in a bit and you can see the course snuggled among the homes.

[xv] SIDS stands for Sudden Infant Death Syndrome

[xvi] Collins English Dictionary -- Complete & Unabridged 10th Edition 2009 © William Collins Sons & Co. Ltd. 1979, 1986 © HarperCollins Publishers 1998, 2000, 2003, 2005, 2006, 2007, 2009